THE CHEROKEE REMOVAL, 1838

Today, over a hundred and thirty years after the Cherokee Removal, the Indians as an entire people still are not assimilated into American Life. As proof that the Indians could have been assimilated long ago the Cherokees are the prime example, not because they alone were adapting even then, but rather because they were the most conspicuously successful, and their removal aroused among white people the greatest outcry of indignation. Over all Indians, the Great Removals cast a pall of discouragement that is renewed with every abrogation by the United States of yet another Indian treaty.

PRINCIPALS

ANDREW JACKSON — President of the United States when the Treaty of Removal was negotiated.

JOHN ROSS — Principal Chief of the Cherokee Nation, who refused to recognize the treaty as valid.

MARTIN VAN BUREN — President of the United States when the treaty was forced into execution.

GENERAL WINFIELD SCOTT — Commander of United States Armed Forces in the removal.

GENERAL JOHN E. WOOL — Inspector General, United States Army, who repeatedly denounced the treaty as a fraud, and was reprimanded by President Jackson.

JOHN F. SCHERMERHORN — United States negotiator of the disputed treaty.

MAJOR WILLIAM M. DAVIS — Enrolling Agent, first United States official to declare the treaty a fraud.

MAJOR RIDGE — A Cherokee chief, the most important signer of the disputed treaty.

JOHN RIDGE — A principal negotiator of the treaty, son of Major Ridge.

ELIAS BOUDINOT — A negotiator of the treaty, a former editor of the *Cherokee Phoenix*, and a cousin of John Ridge.

STAND WATIE — An important member of the Ridge faction, later a brigadier general in the Confederate Army, brother of Boudinot.

John Ross, Principal Chief of the Cherokee Nation from 1828 to 1866. (New York Public Library)

A FOCUS BOOK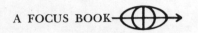

The Cherokee Removal, 1838

An Entire Indian Nation Is Forced Out of Its Homeland

By Glen Fleischmann

FRANKLIN WATTS, INC.
845 Third Avenue, New York, N.Y. 10022

The authors and publisher of the Focus Books wish to acknowledge the helpful editorial suggestions of Professor Richard B. Morris.

Cover photograph:
THE TRAIL OF TEARS, by Robert Lindneux,
from the original oil painting in
Woolaroc Museum, Bartlesville, Oklahoma.

3   4   5   6   7   8   9   10

SNB 531-01024-4

Contents

THE CHEROKEE REMOVAL, 1838

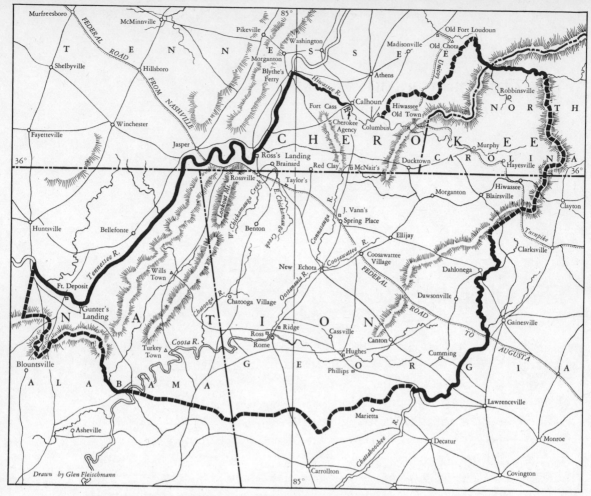

This map of the Cherokee Nation as it was just before the removal shows how extensively its commerce was integrated with that of the surrounding states.

The Cherokee Removal

On May 23, 1838, the United States Army under the command of General Winfield Scott and augmented by militia units from the states of Georgia, Tennessee, Alabama, and North Carolina, to a total strength of 9,494 men, began evicting from their homes 19,000 Cherokee Indians and driving them into stockades. Then, after some unforeseen delays, the Cherokees were removed to lands west of the Mississippi River. In the roundup and in the stockades, and on the journey of over eight hundred miles, 4,000 Cherokees — more than one-fifth of their Nation — died of cholera, dysentery, fever, exposure, improper care of mothers giving birth, and, especially in the aged, loss of the will to survive.

The Cherokees had been living at peace with their neighbors for over two generations. Though some were hunters, trappers, and herb gatherers, they were not warriors or wanderers. Many were planters, tradesmen, herdsmen, craftsmen, artisans, teachers, living in a settled way of life, as they had been advised and encouraged to do, by each successive President of the United States from George Washington to John Quincy Adams. In adapting themselves to an agrarian economy and a settled existence, the Cherokees were succeeding so well that repeatedly they

View of old Cherokee plantation country, looking west from the Joseph Vann house at Spring Place, Georgia. (Photo by author)

were visited by white people of American cities, and by Europeans, curious to observe what seemed to be a cultural and ethnological phenomenon—the assimilation of an Indian nation as it adopted the life-style of the larger, white society around it.

The sudden, forced expulsion of the Cherokees from their homeland was observed with horror by the whole civilized Western world. It was denounced in newspapers in America and in Europe, and in the Congress of the United States. Even in Tennessee, a state that wanted the Indians to remove beyond her borders, Governor Newton Cannon declared the Treaty of Removal an "outrageous document, obviously a fraud, not the proper instrument to accomplish the desired end."

So, in the face of all this opposition, how did it happen, and why?

[4]

Who Were the Evicted?

The Cherokee Indians once claimed — and exercised the right to expel intruders from — a domain roughly estimated at about forty thousand square miles. Bounded on the north by the Ohio River, it included territory that later became most of the states of Kentucky and Tennessee,

Old print depicts early Cherokee chiefs who were brought to visit London in 1730 by Sir Alexander Cuming. As soon as they arrived they were conducted to Windsor where they were present at the installation of Prince William and Lord Chesterfield. (The Smithsonian from Cushing)

The variety and beauty of the old Cherokee country are shown in this view looking northeast from the Joseph Vann house. (Photo by author)

smaller portions of Alabama, Georgia, the Carolinas, Virginia, and West Virginia. Their neighbors were the Shawnee and Miami tribes on the north, Chickasaws and Upper Creeks on the west, Lower Creeks on the south, Catawbas and Wachovias on the east.

Their first known contact with white men occurred in the spring of 1540. Hernando de Soto, the Spanish explorer, and his expedition, after landing on the west coast of Florida, came to a region that his recording secretary called the "Province of Chelaque" (the spoken language of the tribe contained no "r" sound, the word "Cherokee" being an English derivation.)

"These natives," the Spaniard wrote, "cultivate fields of maize, also feed upon roots and herbs which they seek in the fields, and upon wild beasts which they kill with their bows and arrows, and are a very gentle people."

[6]

A century later, when the Atlantic seaboard was being settled and they were first seen by explorers from the English-speaking colonies, the Cherokees were a loosely affiliated group of clans without a principal chief, separate from one another, but they intermarried. Polygamy was common, though not universal. When the male population was reduced by wars, it was not unusual for a man to marry an entire family of sisters. The system was matriarchal, property rights being vested in the women because they cared for the family, the cabin, and cultivated patches of ground, while the men brought in fish and game animals, and furnished protection. Marriages were easily terminated, without ceremony, by husband or wife.

How many Cherokees there were before any census was taken could only be an informed guess. James Adair, a trader, in 1755 estimated that in 64 villages there lived about 16,000 to 17,000 inhabitants.

White Conquest by Infiltration and Treaty Making

The Cherokee clans were said to have made, as early as 1684, a treaty with English-speaking colonists of South Carolina. As the whites began infiltrating westward the clans were forced to unite, for protection and for negotiating treaties that were thrust upon them.

The Cherokee Nation was recognized and its sovereignty guaranteed in all its treaties, first made with colonial governments acting for the British Crown, then with individual states during and immediately after the American War for Independence, and, finally, with the United States after the Federal Government was formed.

But white people, despite these guarantees of sovereignty, continually invaded and settled within the Cherokee domain. The guarantee-

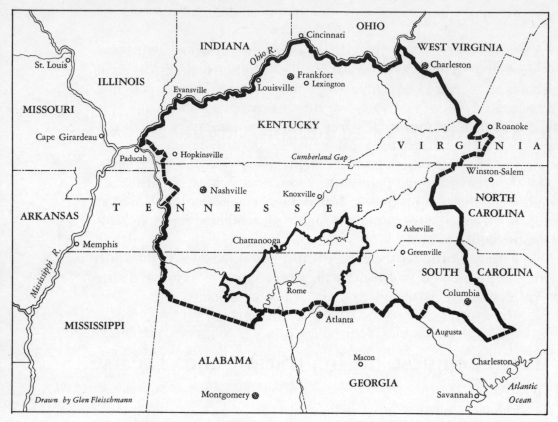

The composite map of the Cherokee domain shows its original area enclosed in heavy outline, then, reduced by land cessions in twenty-eight treaties, its final area in less heavy outline.

ing authority sent armed forces not to expel invaders, as "required" by treaty, but to protect them against the wrath of the invaded. A new treaty would then be negotiated, to "legalize" what had been done illegally, and the Cherokees would have to yield another tract of their land. In twenty-eight treaties (1684, 1721, 1730, 1740, 1755, 1761, 1763, 1767, 1768, 1770, 1771, 1772, 1773, 1775, 1777 two, 1783, 1785, 1791, 1798, 1804,

[8]

1805 two, 1806, 1816 two, 1817, 1819), the Cherokees had thus been forced to relinquish over ninety percent of their original territory.

The Assimilation of an Indian Nation

The Cherokee Nation of Indians in 1838, the year of the removal, held title to a domain in the southeastern states roughly the size of Massachusetts. It lay mostly in Georgia, less in Alabama, still less in Tennessee, and least in North Carolina.

Shrinkage of their territory by so many land cessions had forced them to rely less upon hunting, more upon cultivated crops and the raising of domestic animals.

White traders had for over a century been coming into the country and setting up commercial enterprises, and they had been marrying Cherokee women. Then, as members of the tribe by marriage and adoption, they were allowed to clear tracts of land and become planters.

By the year 1800 the Nation, especially in the lowlands and along the trade routes, included many half-, quarter-, and eighth-bloods, of whom both sexes often found mates among families that were all white. In this changing economy, from hunting and trapping to that of agriculture and trade, children of mixed marriages had an advantage, economically and politically, feeling at home in both cultures. They helped their fathers and grandfathers set the pace for the Nation. As their prosperity increased, mixed marriages became more and more frequent. Whites marrying into the Nation brought family ties that strengthened the bond of blood relationships between the Cherokees and their white neighbors of the surrounding territory.

David Vann, a Cherokee chief. (The Smithsonian from Cushing)

Ethnic Mixtures in the Cherokee Nation

White people who settled in and around the Cherokee Nation were mostly Scottish, Irish, and English. They came from Pennsylvania, Maryland, Virginia, down the Tennessee valley, and from the Carolinas, and coastal Georgia. Many of those from the Savannah and Charleston areas were of a higher social class than were those who came through Tennessee, and, if not wealthy, they had the traditions of wealth, a better education, and some property for a start. Younger sons were often given a few slaves, a little money, and sent into the wilderness where, with

[10]

industry and sound labor management, they could carve out a plantation. As their slaves bred and multiplied, more land was cleared to utilize and support the expanding labor supply.

Cherokee families of mixed ancestry inherited through the white male line such names as Blackburn, Taylor, Coodey, Vann, Charlton, Saunders, McNair, Blakelock, Nellums, Blythe, Shelton, Walker, Parks, Ross, Melton, Henson, Woodhall, Pack, Rogers, Townsend, Ward, Mayfield, Still, Martin, Bruce, Waters, Lowrey, Smith, Eldridge, Starr, MacGregor, Brown, Davis, Richardson, McDaniel, McDonald, Gunter, McCoy, Daniel, Baldridge, Petit, Bolinger, England, Montgomery, Wilson, MacDowell. . . .

Growth of Agriculture, Crafts, and Commerce

Plantations grew and multiplied. Commerce demanded better, faster communications and transport.

A network of roads and turnpikes needed houses of accommodation for travelers, and a different set of public houses for the rougher trade of drovers and freighters, with pens for cattle, swine, sheep, and horses, on the way to market.

This changing economy is most evident in the Cherokee national inventory of 1825, which listed: cattle 17,531; horses 7,653; swine 47,732; sheep 2,556; goats 430, looms 752; spinning wheels 2,486; wagons 72; plows 921; sawmills 10; gristmills 31; blacksmith shops 62; cotton machines 8; stores 9; schools 12; ferries 18; turnpike gates 6.

Cherokee Wealth Compared with that of Whites

Ownership of slaves is one means of comparing the wealth of Cherokees with that of their white neighbors living in country nearest like their own. A prime field hand (between the ages of fifteen and thirty-five) cost $1,000 to $1,500 or more. A skilled carpenter, a brickmaker or bricklayer, a tanner and leatherworker, a blacksmith, cost $1,500 to $2,000.

The Cherokee census of 1835 listed: Cherokees (full bloods and mixed bloods) 16,532; whites intermarried with Cherokees 201; slaves 1,592. (The Cherokees showed no increase over estimates in previous years because several parties had been induced by the United States Government to emigrate west of the Mississippi.) The Georgia census was taken at the decade, but the figures for 1830 (five years would bring increases, but would not necessarily alter the ratio of white to slave population) in counties just across the Chattahoochee River from the Cherokees, showed: for Gwinnett County, whites 10,938; slaves 2,274; free colored 8: for De Kalb County, whites 8,375; slaves 1,654; free colored 18.

The ratio of slaves to Cherokees (and their white mates) was about 1 to 10.5. In Gwinnett County the ratio of slaves to whites was 1 to 4.08; in De Kalb 1 to 5. But in the Nation, unlike the Georgia counties, there was some mountainous country where a plantation economy was not feasible, and cultivated acreages were small and scattered. Mountaineers, white or Indian, did not own slaves.

A plantation, in white or Indian territory, that employed 100 slaves was considered very large. The Cherokee census of 1835 listed Joseph Vann as the owner of 110 slaves; George Waters 100; John Martin 69; many had more than 20 but less than 50. John Ross (Principal Chief) was far down the list with only 19. His brother Lewis had 41. The num-

[12]

The Joseph Vann manor house. (Photo by author)

ber of slaves employed by other Cherokees (again like the whites) ranged downward to a single household servant or laborer, depending upon their need, acreage under cultivation, and wealth. In ratio to total population, few families, white or Cherokee, owned any slaves.

The more prosperous Cherokees were already on equal terms economically and socially with their white counterparts across the Chattahoochee. They lived in roomy, comfortable houses of brick, frame, and stone.

Joseph Vann's manor house, a red-brick Georgian colonial designed by a Philadelphia architect, was built as long ago as 1799. It was finished with such details as carved mantelpieces, a floating stairway in the center hall, and a two-story portico. (Restored after years of neglect this house can be seen today, at Spring Place, Georgia.)

Major Ridge had a fine manor house on his plantation in the Coosa

[13]

Valley. (It is now the residence of the local plant manager of the Celanese Corporation, at Rome, Georgia.)

John Ross lived at Rossville, Georgia, in a house that had been erected by his father, Daniel Ross, who owned a tannery and a trading post. (This house also stands today, fully restored, and open to the public.)

These Cherokees had their furniture and furnishings brought out from the Eastern cities. They wore clothing of the same kind and cut worn by whites of their economic level. They drove good horses, hitched to fine carriages. They sent their sons and daughters to schools in the Nation, then to academies and seminaries in South Carolina, Tennessee, and Connecticut.

Cherokee Literacy, Education, and Religions

In 1801 the Moravian Brethren, in collaboration with Cherokee leaders, had opened a school at Spring Place. Other missionary organizations followed and opened more schools. The Cherokees erected the buildings. The Moravians, the Methodists, the Presbyterians, the Congregationalists, the Baptists, provided the teachers, and conducted church services on Sundays for all who wished to attend. In 1817, Brainerd Mission, a coeducational boarding school, was founded.

The children of wealthier Cherokees had at first been educated by tutors in their own schoolrooms on the plantation. But as the Nation's schools were established, these children, whose fathers were by necessity all politically involved, were sent to school with the children of less affluent families, to set an example and solidify the Nation to resist outside pressures.

In 1821, Sequoya, a Cherokee of mixed ancestry, known to the whites as George Guess, or Gist, perfected an alphabet, or syllabary, which enabled those who spoke only Cherokee to read and write in their

Sequoya, a Cherokee Indian of mixed ancestry, perfected an alphabet, or syllabary, of his tribe's language. Below, Sequoya's alphabet in print. (The Smithsonian from Cushing)

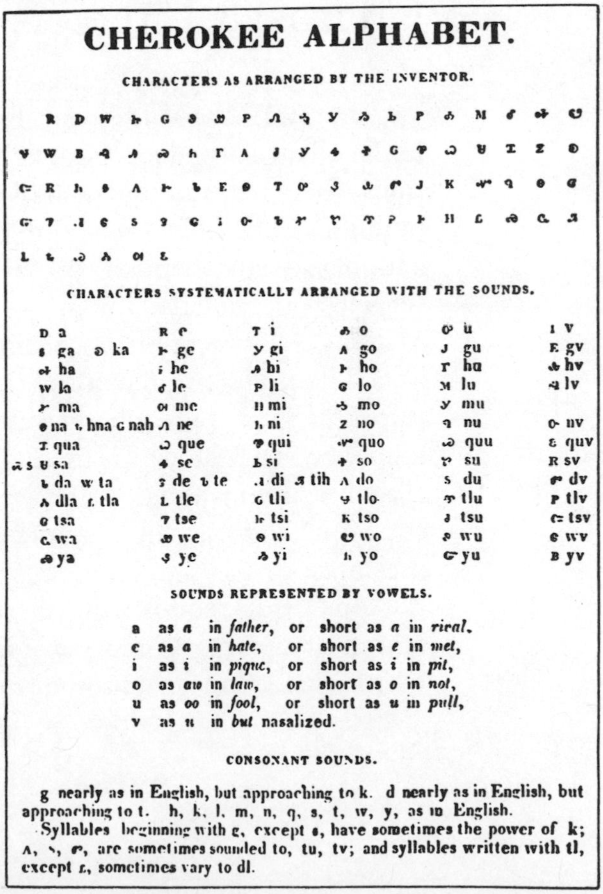

CHEROKEE ALPHABET.

CHARACTERS AS ARRANGED BY THE INVENTOR.

Ꭱ Ꭰ Ꮃ Ꭸ Ꮐ Ꭷ Ꮺ Ꮅ Ꮑ Ꮌ Ꭹ Ꭿ Ꮟ Ꮲ Ꭳ Ꮇ Ꮄ Ꭽ Ꮼ

Ꮰ Ꮤ Ᏼ Ꮔ Ꮽ Ꮹ Ꮒ Ꮁ Ꭺ Ꭻ Ꮍ Ꮞ Ꮠ Ꮳ Ꮘ Ꮗ Ꮜ Ꮖ Ꮓ Ꮻ

Ꮸ Ꮢ Ꮵ Ꭶ Ꮩ Ꮀ Ꮦ Ꭼ Ꮎ Ꭲ Ꭴ Ᏸ Ꮿ Ꮫ Ꭻ Ꮶ Ꮙ Ꮔ Ꮻ Ꮾ

Ᏻ Ꮴ Ꮧ Ꮯ Ꮪ Ꮷ Ꮆ Ꮟ Ꮕ Ꮣ Ꮉ Ꮏ Ꮱ Ꮭ Ꮂ Ꮋ Ꮬ Ꮿ Ꮹ Ꮨ

Ꮮ Ꮤ Ꮚ Ꮩ Ꮊ Ꮛ

CHARACTERS SYSTEMATICALLY ARRANGED WITH THE SOUNDS.

Ꭰ a	Ꭱ e	Ꭲ i	Ꭳ o	Ꭴ u	Ꭵ v
Ꭶ ga Ꭷ ka	Ꭸ ge	Ꭹ gi	Ꭺ go	Ꭻ gu	Ꭼ gv
Ꭽ ha	Ꭾ he	Ꭿ hi	Ꮀ ho	Ꮁ hu	Ꮂ hv
Ꮃ la	Ꮄ le	Ꮅ li	Ꮆ lo	Ꮇ lu	Ꮈ lv
Ꮉ ma	Ꮊ me	Ꮋ mi	Ꮌ mo	Ꮍ mu	
Ꮎ na Ꮏ hna Ꮐ nah	Ꮑ ne	Ꮒ ni	Ꮓ no	Ꮔ nu	Ꮕ nv
Ꮖ qua	Ꮗ que	Ꮘ qui	Ꮙ quo	Ꮚ quu	Ꮛ quv
Ꮝ s Ꮜ sa	Ꮞ se	Ꮟ si	Ꮠ so	Ꮡ su	Ꮢ sv
Ꮣ da Ꮤ ta	Ꮥ de Ꮦ te	Ꮧ di Ꮨ tih	Ꮩ do	Ꮪ du	Ꮫ dv
Ꮬ dla Ꮭ tla	Ꮮ tle	Ꮯ tli	Ꮰ tlo	Ꮱ tlu	Ꮲ tlv
Ꮳ tsa	Ꮴ tse	Ꮵ tsi	Ꮶ tso	Ꮷ tsu	Ꮸ tsv
Ꮹ wa	Ꮺ we	Ꮻ wi	Ꮼ wo	Ꮽ wu	Ꮾ wv
Ꮿ ya	Ᏸ ye	Ᏹ yi	Ᏺ yo	Ᏻ yu	Ᏼ yv

SOUNDS REPRESENTED BY VOWELS.

a as *a* in *father*, or short as *a* in *rival*,
e as *a* in *hate*, or short as *e* in *met*,
i as *i* in *pique*, or short as *i* in *pit*,
o as *aw* in *law*, or short as *o* in *not*,
u as *oo* in *fool*, or short as *u* in *pull*,
v as *u* in *but* nasalized.

CONSONANT SOUNDS.

g nearly as in English, but approaching to k. d nearly as in English, but approaching to t. h, k, l, m, n, q, s, t, w, y, as in English.

Syllables beginning with g, except Ꭶ, have sometimes the power of k; Ꭺ, Ꮝ, Ꮫ, are sometimes sounded to, tu, tv; and syllables written with tl, except Ꮭ, sometimes vary to dl.

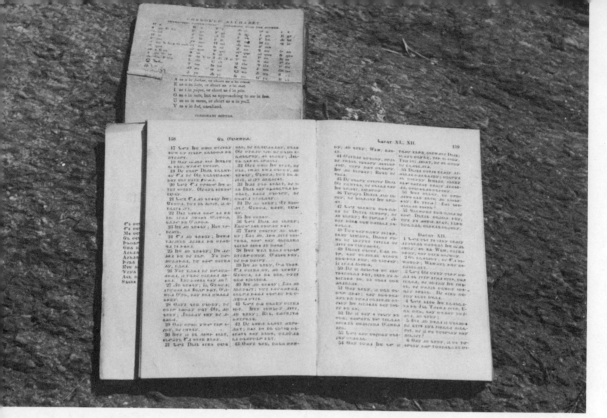

This Indian Bible and hymnbook was among many publications in the Cherokee language. (Charles Phelps Cushing)

own language. It had never, up to this time, been expressed in graphic form. Although he could not himself read the English language from which he devised it, the syllabary was practical and easily learned. It had eighty-five characters as compared with the twenty-six English letters, but each character had only one sound, so there was no confusion in learning it. Younger people, who had been to school, did not need it, but many of their elders found it useful.

On February 21, 1828, the *Cherokee Phoenix*, a four-page weekly newspaper printed half in English and half in Sequoya's alphabet (the type had been specially cast in Boston), began publication at the Cherokee capital of New Echota (near the present site of Calhoun, Georgia). In this paper the Cherokees read local and world news, market prices, and, in serialized form, their new constitution, which had been adopted by the National Council the year before. Its press also produced hymnbooks, gospels, and pamphlets, in the Cherokee language, with Cherokees, at first supervised by the missionaries, doing the writing, translating, editing, typesetting, printing, and binding. A printer had been hired from outside, but as native apprentices learned the trade they took over operation of the press. The plant was owned by the Nation. The *Phoenix* had subscribers also in the states and in foreign countries where the Cherokees had aroused much interest, in government and among naturalists and students of human relations.

By 1830 about two hundred Cherokees could read and write English, a great many more could speak it, and by 1832 it was said that about half the Nation could read and write in Sequoya's alphabet.

The Cherokee Government

The Cherokees had begun in 1809 to enact laws by National Council. In 1819 they adopted a commission government, with legislative powers vested in a committee of thirteen elected members. In 1820 the Nation was apportioned into eight districts, each represented in the Council by four salaried members chosen by popular election every two years. On July 26, 1827, a convention of delegates duly authorized by the Cherokee people in assembly at New Echota, ratified and adopted a new constitution patterned after that of the United States. The National Council then became a legislative body composed of two houses comparable to the United States Congress.

The Principal Chief and the Second Chief, hitherto chosen by the National Committee, and then by the National Council, were now to be elected by popular vote.

The Fatal Flaw

Cherokee aspirations in and for their homeland were doomed as far back as March 4, 1789, when the United States Government declared its own Constitution was now in effect. Ratifications had been accepted from certain states (Georgia, January 2, 1788; South Carolina, May 23, 1788; Virginia, June 26, 1788) whose boundaries had been drawn through the Cherokee Nation as if it did not exist, and even though the Federal Government and the states themselves recognized by treaty the sovereignty of the Cherokee Nation. On November 21, 1789, North Carolina ratified the Constitution, and its boundaries were accepted as drawn — through the Cherokee Nation. Later, the new states of Kentucky, Alabama, and Tennessee were formed, admitted to the Union, and their boundaries accepted, even though they too ignored Cherokee sovereignty.

Government Ambiguity or Duplicity?

The Jefferson Administration, while encouraging the Cherokees to strengthen their government and develop as a civilized people, with guarantees of their permanent occupancy of their homeland, made (in 1802) an agreement with Georgia in which that state "relinquished" its claim to lands extending west to the Mississippi River (lands owned and occupied by Cherokees, Creeks, and Chickasaws, and guaranteed to them by

Thomas Jefferson, whose friendliness and goodwill toward Cherokee aspirations were never doubted, yet whose administration signed the agreement with Georgia in 1802, which made the Cherokee removal almost inevitable.

treaty "for as long as the sun shines and rivers flow"). For this "surrender" of "rights" it never had, Georgia received a cash payment and a promise that the Federal Government would, "as early as the same can be peaceably obtained, on reasonable terms," extinguish the Indian (Cherokee and Creek) title within the state's boundaries.

The Jefferson Administration made, in 1803, the Louisiana Purchase, which most American citizens believed, and still believe, added a great new territory to the United States. It did not. By its terms the United States obtained, not the land, but simply the "exclusive right [hitherto claimed by France] to purchase" the land from the people who occupied it, the western tribes of Indians — if or when they chose to sell it. After the Louisiana Purchase, the Federal Government began trying to induce the Cherokees to exchange their homeland for a new domain west of the Mississippi.

In 1805 and 1806, a few Cherokees did emigrate, but their position in the West was not secured until their people in the East ceded enough territory to pay for land owned by the western tribes.

For the next two decades and more the United States Government: 1) encouraged the Cherokees to believe they could remain in their homeland forever; 2) reaffirmed its obligation to extinguish the Indian title within the State of Georgia; 3) told the Cherokees it could not protect their sovereignty in the East; and 4) told the State of Georgia the Cherokees did not have to move if they did not want to.

These contradictory policies were made not by different or alternating administrations, but were stated and restated by the same administrations.

The Pressure Increases on the Cherokees

The State of Georgia, after ten years of waiting, grew impatient, began pressing the Federal Government to discharge its obligation. After twenty years it began harassing the Cherokees, to induce them to remove "voluntarily." But the Federal Government, though continually trying to obtain from the Cherokees a treaty of removal, assured them of their continued sovereignty for as long as they chose to remain.

Andrew Jackson, elected in 1828, President of the United States, promptly ended this ambiguity and vacillation by the Federal Government. He was quoted as having told state officials of Georgia, concerning the Cherokees:

"Build a fire under them. When it gets hot enough, they'll move."

The Georgia Legislature, on December 19, 1828, enacted a "law" that preempted within the state all sovereignty of the Cherokees hitherto recognized and guaranteed by all treaties; prohibited the Cherokee Council from assembling within the state; and declared that henceforth "no Indian or descendent of Indian," no matter how slight the fraction of Indian ancestry, "shall be deemed a competent witness in any dispute or litigation involving a white person." The state thus imposed its jurisdiction over the Cherokees, but denied them any protection of Georgia laws.

[20]

Chief John Ross, on January 21, 1829, presented to the Secretary of War a statement of grievances and a petition for redress.

President Jackson, on April 18, replied through the Secretary of War, advising the Cherokee delegation that their sovereignty and safety in their homeland could no longer be guaranteed; that by winning the War for Independence, the United States acquired title to lands thus relinquished by Great Britain, "of which the Cherokee domain was a part." Also, that in the treaty with the Cherokees (as allies of Great Britain), the United States "took them into protection as a dependent people." The President then affirmed the "sovereignty of each State over all the land within its boundaries, be its occupants white or Indian."

The Supreme Court Reaffirms Cherokee Sovereignty

The United States Supreme Court, at the January session 1832, in a test case, *Worcester versus the State of Georgia*, denied all claims of the United States and of individual states to sovereignty over the Cherokee Nation.

"The Principle of Discovery," the Court explained, "by which a discoverer took possession of discovered territory in the name of his country, did not convey ownership nor impair the right of the occupants to sell or not to sell their land." The discovering nation merely obtained the "exclusive right of purchase." No nation had ever contended otherwise. This "Principle of Discovery" was recognized and agreed to by all nations of the earth because it was in their interest to do so. After the War for Independence, Great Britain relinquished to her former colonies, not Indian lands (which she never owned), but the "exclusive right to purchase them."

[21]

The Supreme Court explained also that in making treaties with the Cherokee Nation, the United States used words that were "internationally understood as having definite meanings." The words "treaty" and "nation" were "of our own choosing and meant to apply to all nations in the same way." In being a "dependent nation," the Cherokees did not lose their sovereignty: to "take them into protection" was not meant to imply destruction of the "protected."

The President Defies the Court

President Jackson was quoted (by the Hon. George N. Briggs, member of Congress from Massachusetts) as having remarked, in reference to the Supreme Court ruling:

"John Marshall has made his decision, now let him enforce it."

The State of Georgia intensified its harassment of the Cherokees. It confiscated Cherokee national property (school buildings, council houses, printing plant), also the property of certain chiefs who opposed removal. It sent surveyors into the Nation, and instituted lotteries to distribute Cherokee property. Unofficial "pony clubs" were permitted, exempt from prosecution, to raid Cherokee plantations and drive off livestock, to kidnap slaves in the fields, and to destroy crops.

Andrew Jackson, as painted by Samuel Waldo, probably looked like this at the time of the Creek War, when Major John Ross served as his adjutant.

John Marshall, Chief Justice of the Supreme Court when that body affirmed the sovereignty of the Cherokee Nation, within whose boundaries, therefore, the laws of any state could have no legal force.

The Federal Government assisted Georgia in its policy of harassment by withholding annuities (due the Cherokees for past land cessions). It ordered Federal troops (in the Nation to protect the Cherokees against invaders) to prevent Cherokees from working gold deposits (gold had been discovered at Dahlonega). It assigned an enrolling and appraising agent to persuade Cherokee families and individuals to exchange their property for its equivalent in the West. Teams of commissioners were sent into the Nation, one after another, to persuade the National Council to accept a treaty of removal. Inducements were offered to the more influential chiefs, factions were encouraged to oppose their government. But the nearest thing to a dissident party that could be found was the Ridge family and their adherents.

The Ridges differed from John Ross only in believing they would have to move anyhow, so they had better accept the best terms they could get and emigrate.

[23]

The Disputed Treaty

The Reverend John F. Schermerhorn (appointed February 11, 1835), Commissioner for the President, in the spring and summer of 1835 was carrying on negotiations with the Cherokees. His fellow Commissioner, William Carroll (appointed April 2), being in ill health, Schermerhorn continued alone.

At the October Council, meeting at Red Clay, Tennessee, he submitted yet another treaty of removal. It was rejected. His proposal then of further negotiations on the spot was rejected, because without further instructions from the President he could offer no terms other than those rejected. He then challenged Principal Chief Ross's authority to speak for the Council and its constituents. This challenge also was rejected, the Ridge group concurring to make it unanimous.

Mr. Schermerhorn, reporting to the Secretary of War, Lewis Cass, on these proceedings (Senate Document 120, 25th Congress, 2nd session, p. 124), wrote:

"I have pressed Ross so hard by the course I have adopted that although he got the Council to pass a resolution declaring they would not treat on the basis of the $5,000,000, yet he has been forced to bring the Nation to agree to a treaty, here or at Washington. They have used every effort to get by me and get to Washington again this winter. They dare not yet do it. You will perceive that Ridge and his friends have taken apparently a strange course. I believe he began to be discouraged in contending with the power of Ross; and perhaps also considerations of personal safety have had their influence, but the Lord is able to overrule all things for good."

John Ross and his delegation (John Ridge, Lewis Ross, and John Martin), contrary to Schermerhorn's confident statement that they dare not leave the Nation, did so dare and proceed to Washington.

[24]

On December 29, 1835, at New Echota, a treaty was concluded by Schermerhorn and signed by a group of twenty Cherokees.

Mr. Schermerhorn wrote to the Secretary of War, December 30:

"I have the extreme pleasure to announce to you that yesterday I concluded a treaty. Ross, after the treaty, is prostrate. The power of the Nation is taken from him, as well as the money, and the treaty will give general satisfaction."

On December 31, Mr. Schermerhorn wrote to the Commissioner of Indian Affairs a full account of the proceedings.

John Ross, Principal Chief of the Cherokees

John Ross at this time was forty-five years old. He was described by an Army officer as of "medium height, slender, with blue eyes and brown hair" that showed "no signs of thinning with the advance of years," and that he could have passed as a "prosperous business man of Boston, New York, or Philadelphia."

Born October 2, 1790, at Tah-na-hoo-yah (meaning "Logs-in-the-water") on the Coosa River in what later became the community of Tur-keytown, Etowah County, Alabama, he now lived with his family in a tiny log cabin at Red Clay, Tennessee. His plantation, at Head of Coosa, near Rome, Georgia, had been confiscated by the State of Georgia and placed in the lottery distributing Cherokee property. The Ross family were evicted by the "fortunate drawer," and the Georgia Guard.

John Ross's great-grandfather on his mother's side, William Shorey, had been an interpreter for the British Army at Fort Loudon, where he married a full-blood Cherokee woman named Ghi-goo-ie (meaning "Sweetheart"). Their daughter Anne Shorey married John McDonald, from Inverness, Scotland, who had set up a store at Fort Loudon for a mercantile firm of Charleston, South Carolina. Their daughter Molly

Chief John Ross's house (from an old print). Built in 1797, and now fully restored after years of neglect, it is maintained and administered by the John Ross House Association, Inc., at Rossville, Georgia.

McDonald married Daniel Ross, a Scotsman from Sutherlandshire, who had brought a shipment of merchandise down from Baltimore. Captured by Indians, his life was saved by his future father-in-law. Daniel Ross later established a store, a tannery, and the town of Rossville on Chicamauga Creek, near the foot of Lookout Mountain.

Daniel and Molly McDonald Ross had nine children: Jennie, Lewis, Elizabeth, John, Susannah, Andrew, Anna, Margaret, and Maria. Daniel Ross accumulated a good library, built a small schoolhouse on his grounds, and employed as a teacher one John Barbour Davis. Children of neighboring Cherokees also were taught at this school.

Lewis and John Ross were later sent to a school in Kingston, Tennessee, conducted by the Reverend Gideon Blackburn, Presbyterian minister, then to an academy at Maryville, Tennessee. At the Kingston school a classmate of John Ross was Sam Houston, who remained a lifelong friend and lived among the Cherokees at various times before and after being Governor of Tennessee. Houston's second wife was a Cherokee.

When, in 1809, Return J. Meigs, United States Indian Agent, needed an emissary for a conciliatory mission to the Western Cherokees, he chose John Ross, then only nineteen years old.

John Ross married, in 1812, a young widow with one daughter. His bride was Elizabeth Brown Henley, daughter of James Brown, Treasurer of the Cherokee Nation. Known to the Cherokees as "Quatie," she was said to be a woman of "strong deep character and of noble mind."

In the War of 1812 between the United States and England, John Ross, with the rank of major, served as adjutant to General Andrew Jackson. In the War of 1813-1814 against the Creek "Red Sticks," John Ross again served under Jackson.

John Ross as businessman, first was in partnership with Timothy Meigs, son of the United States Agent to the Cherokees. Ross and Meigs

Elizabeth ("Quatie") Brown Henley Ross, wife of Chief John Ross and mother of five Ross children. She died on February 1, 1839, as their emigrant party approached Little Rock.

established a store near the agency on the Hiwassee River. When John sold his share in this business to his elder brother Lewis, he then built his own store, warehouse, and boat dock (which became known as Ross's Landing), on the Tennessee River, about three miles from his family home at Rossville. In later years, he sold this business and his house at Rossville (which he had bought from the family estate) to Nicholas Dalton Scales, who had married Ross's niece, Maria Coody. Ross had then bought the plantation (from which subsequently his family was evicted by a "fortunate drawer") at Head of Coosa, near Rome, Georgia.

Elected in 1817 to the Cherokee National Committee, Ross became, in 1819, its President, a position third in importance in the Nation, outranked only by the Principal Chief, Pathkiller, and the Second Chief, Charles Hicks. He was then twenty-eight years old.

John Ross, from 1819 until the treaty of December 1835 (the document now under dispute), had successfully opposed every attempt by the United States to secure any further land cessions from the Cherokees.

His position as Principal Chief he owed partly to the fact that after the death of Charles Hicks (newly elected to succeed the late Pathkiller), William Hicks, who then sought to succeed his brother, had been, according to the Hicks dossier at the United States Department of War, "observed too much in the company of Georgia politicians."

The elections, in 1828, of John Ross as Principal Chief of the Cherokee Nation, and Andrew Jackson as President of the United States, inaugurated no new clash of personalities. In the peace treaty terminating the Creek War, Jackson took "by mistake" as part of the Creek indemnity four million acres of Cherokee land. Major John Ross, Jackson's adjutant, joined in the Cherokee protest which induced the War Department to rectify the "mistake." Ross had never trusted Jackson since.

John Ross knew personally every United States politician of his time who sympathized with Cherokee aspirations: Henry Clay of Kentucky, David Crockett and Sam Houston of Tennessee, Daniel Webster and Edward Everett of Massachusetts, Horace Everett of Vermont, Peleg

[28]

David Crockett of Tennessee, who had lived among the Cherokees, failed of reelection to Congress because he publicly and officially encouraged their hopes of retaining their homeland.

Sam Houston, schoolmate of John Ross and a lifelong friend, lived with the Cherokees before and after he served in Congress and as governor of Tennessee. His second wife was a Cherokee woman.

Sprague of Maine, Theodore Frelinghuysen of New Jersey, Henry A. Wise of Virginia, and many others. His consulting with Congressmen and with news editors did not endear him to those officials of the Jackson Administration with whom he had to deal. But Ross did nothing in that respect which they had not been doing for years in trying to bypass and undercut him with his people and with members of the Cherokee National Council. In this he was merely using their tactics, but defensively, not aggressively.

Members of the Ridge Faction

Major Ridge was another of the Cherokee chiefs who had served under General Jackson in the War against the Creeks. Now a planter, in the Coosa Valley, he was considered the most eloquent orator in the National Council. A Cherokee patriot since childhood, he was the one most responsible for getting a law enacted providing the death penalty for any-

The Ridge ("one who walks on higher ground and sees further than others"), known also as Major Ridge, was a regional chief who served under Andrew Jackson in the Creek War. Highest-ranking signer of the disputed treaty of 1835, he was quoted as saying as he took the pen: "I know I am signing my own death warrant." (The Smithsonian from Cushing)

John Ridge, son of Major Ridge, and himself a member of the Cherokee National Council, was not present at the negotiation and signing of the disputed treaty, but agreed to it later in Washington.

one signing away Cherokee land without authorization from the people. When, in 1808, Doublehead and other chiefs ceded a large tract north of the Tennessee River, without authorization, their executioners were Major Ridge himself and John Rogers (great great grandfather of the late Will Rogers).

John, son of Major Ridge, also had a plantation in the Coosa Valley, was a member of the Council, very active, and of growing influence. His advanced education he had received at an academy in Cornwall, Connecticut, and there he had married a white girl, daughter of an instructor.

Elias Boudinot, a cousin of John Ridge, had attended the same acad-

Elias Boudinot, editor of the Cherokee Phoenix, *and later a prominent signer of the disputed treaty of 1835. (New York Public Library)*

Harriet Gold Boudinot, wife of Elias, daughter of a white family in Cornwall, Connecticut, where her husband had attended an academy. She died before the journey west, leaving her husband with five children, and is buried at the site of New Echota, the Cherokee capital at that time, near the present town of Calhoun, Georgia (New York Public Library)

Robert Bruce Ross, grandson of Chief Ross, at the grave of Harriet Gold Boudinot at the site of the old Cherokee capital. (Courtesy, Robert Sparks Walker)

Stand Watie, brother of Elias Boudinot, and a member of the Ridge faction, was later a general in the Confederate Army.

emy with John, and had also married a white girl there. He became an assistant editor of the *Cherokee Phoenix*, then editor, and, finally, ex-editor when his editorial policies conflicted with the policies and aims of John Ross in trying to hold the Cherokees in a united front against removal.

Another member of the Ridge faction was Stand Watie, brother of Elias Boudinot. Still others included William A. Davis, A. Smith, S. W. Bell, and J. West, all Council members, who shared with the Ridges a fear of being dispossessed by the Georgians and becoming homeless wanderers in their own land.

The lesser of two evils, these Cherokees believed, would be to drive the best bargain they could with the United States, and resettle in the West.

[33]

The Principal Chief is "Deposed"

John Ross, arriving in Washington with his fellow delegates (John Ridge, Lewis Ross, and John Martin) while unknown to him the treaty was being negotiated and signed at New Echota, was cordially received at the War Department. He was given an audience with the President. Conversations were carried on with Government officials, who obviously regarded him as the accredited representative of his people. The bad news, however, at least from his viewpoint, was already on its way to Washington. When it arrived, the conferences were abruptly terminated, with the announcement that further talk on the subject of a treaty would be superfluous.

In the meantime Second Chief Lowrey, who had refused to participate in the treaty making, had organized a crew of assistants in the Nation and they were collecting signatures for a protest against it.

Schermerhorn's delegation accompanied the Commissioner to Washington, where they were joined by John Ridge (who thereby deserted the Ross delegation) when he saw that his father and his cousin, Elias Boudinot, had signed the treaty. This delegation and Government officials were completing details of the treaty when Chief Ross received from Second Chief Lowrey the petition of protest signed by 15,964 Cherokees.

The Commissioner of Indian Affairs replied (March 9) to John Ross, concerning the petition, that the President did not recognize the existence of any legal government in the Cherokee Nation East.

[34]

The Treaty Is Declared a Fraud

Commissioner Schermerhorn had specifically requested (September 10, 1835) approval of a plan "to conclude a treaty with only a part of the Nation, should one with the whole be found impracticable, and force the remainder to comply."

Secretary of War Lewis Cass had promptly (letter September 26) advised Mr. Schermerhorn that President Jackson was "absolutely opposed to any such procedure." If conclusion of a treaty upon "fair and open terms" should prove impossible, the Commissioner must abandon the project and "leave the Nation to the consequences of its own stubbornness.... The interest of the whole must not be sacrificed to the cupidity of the few." Any treaty to be concluded "must be one that would stand the test of the most rigid scrutiny."

Now the Secretary of War received a letter, dated March 5, 1836, from Major William M. Davis, an officer assigned to enroll Cherokee emigrants willing to move west. Davis charged that Schermerhorn had done precisely what he had been told not to do: that the treaty was made by "a small minority of no more than 300 to 350 persons," that Schermerhorn had taken no roll call because it would have revealed the small number, and that "nineteen-twentieths" of the Cherokees would repudiate the treaty.

News of this letter somehow leaked out to the newspapers, a Congressional committee demanded a look at the letter, then demanded an investigation. The investigating officer sent down there confirmed the Davis charges, and warned of increasing tension, in the Cherokee Nation and in Georgia counties many of whose inhabitants had long coveted Cherokee land.

Cherokee Agency, East.
5th March 1836

Sir,

In 1831 I had the honor to receive from your hands the appointment of Enrolling and Appraising Agent in the removal of the Cherokees west of the Mississippi. Since which time I have faithfully discharged my duty here without complaint or fault finding of me, from any quarter white or Red. I speak of this with more pride and pleasure, as I stand alone upon this point, among those with whom I have been associated here. I have been thus fortunate because I have been uniformly friendly and conciliatory to these people in all things— advocating the policy of the Administration with firmness but always with mildness and friendship— showing the greatest respect for their feelings and sympathy for their distressed situa=tion, and in my intercourse here I have known no party, but have been equally

Major William M. Davis was the first U.S. official to declare the Cherokee treaty of removal a fraud. These are the first and last pages of a 27-page letter he wrote on the subject to Secretary of War Lewis Cass.

I should expose and arraign him
before the President.

With very great respect
I have the honor to
subscribe myself
Your most obt Sevt

Wm. M. Davis

Hon.
    Lewis Cass
Secry of War
    Washington City

The Treaty Is Ratified

On May 23, 1836, the treaty was ratified by the margin of a single vote and despite some formidable opposition led by Senators Webster and Clay. And it was promptly signed by President Jackson. By its terms the Cherokees were allowed two years in which to tidy up their affairs in their homeland and move west of the Mississippi. They were to receive in exchange 13,800,000 acres in the West and $5,000,000 to pay all depredation claims and the cost of moving.

A commission, composed of Wilson Lumpkin (former Governor of Georgia) and William Carroll (former Governor of Tennessee), was appointed, June 7, by President Jackson to supervise execution of the treaty.

The Cherokee petition of protest against the treaty was submitted by John Ross, June 21, to both Houses of Congress, which adjourned, July 4, without having considered it.

Georgians Demand Protection

Rumor with its "thousand tongues" one evening spread like prairie fire through Georgia counties adjacent to the Cherokee Nation. Georgians fled in all directions, yelling: "Massacre! Cherokees on the warpath!"

But the scare spent itself without anyone knowing who started it, or where it started. Cherokees only smiled, and repeated a line from Proverbs: " 'The wicked flee when no man pursueth, but the righteous are bold as a lion.' "

Governor Schley, of Georgia, appealed to the Secretary of War to protect Georgia citizens and to "disarm the hostile" Cherokee.

[38]

General John Ellis Wool, Inspector General of the United States Army, was ordered, July 30, to take command of Federal troops in the Cherokee Nation (stationed there to protect the Cherokees against invasion by whites), then to call up volunteers to expand his total force to 2,450 men, and collect all Cherokee arms. He was instructed to "apply force only if hostilities are initiated by the Cherokees." Surrender of arms was to be complete, but "voluntary," as "evidence of peaceful intentions." There was no legal justification for taking them. The Cherokee guns were not military weapons (renounced by treaty in exchange for protection by the United States Army), but private property, which had been used for hunting and to protect livestock from wild animals.

The disarming was completed by September 1.

Brigadier General R. G. Dunlap, at the disbanding of his Eastern Tennessee Volunteers, made a speech, copies of which he released to the press. Among other things, he said:

"I visited all the posts within the first three States and gave the Cherokees (the whites needed none) all the protection in my power. . . . My course has excited the hatred of a few of the lawless rabble in Georgia who have long played the part of unfeeling petty tyrants, and that to the disgrace of the proud character of gallant soldiers and good citizens. I had determined that I would never dishonor the Tennessee arms by aiding to carry into execution at the point of the bayonet a treaty made by a lean minority against the will and authority of the Cherokee people. . . . I soon discovered that the Indians had not the most distant thought of war with the United States, notwithstanding the common rights of humanity and justice had been denied them."

Cherokee Opposition to the Treaty Solidifies

John Ross and the Council, in late summer, composed another petition to the United States Government.

General Wool sent it on the the War Department.

Secretary of War Lewis Cass wrote back that he had been instructed by President Jackson to express the "shock" he felt at learning that a high officer of the Army had forwarded "a document so odious and insulting to his Commander-in-Chief, and through him, to the people of the United States."

General Wool, despite this reprimand, continued to send reports unfavorable to the treaty. To Adjutant General Roger Jones, in Washington, he wrote, February 18:

"I called them [the Cherokees] together and made a short speech. It

Lewis Cass, Secretary of War, had the unpleasant duty of passing on to President Jackson, from officers in the field, their frequent reports denouncing the Cherokee treaty as a fraud.

John Ellis Wool, Inspector General, U.S. Army, was reprimanded by President Jackson for transmitting Cherokee protests and reporting unfavorably on the treaty.

is, however, vain to talk to a people almost universally opposed to the treaty and who maintain that they never made such a treaty. So determined are they in their opposition that not one of those who were present and voted at the Council held a day or two since, however poor or destitute, would receive rations or clothing from the United States lest they might compromise themselves in regard to the treaty. These same people (many of whom had been dispossessed of their property by invading Georgians), as well as those in the mountains of North Carolina, during the summer past, preferred living upon the roots and sap of trees rather than receive provisions from the United States, and thousands, I have been informed, had no other food for weeks. Many have said they will die before they will leave their country."

John Ross was now virtually without opposition among his people in their homeland.

Commissioners Wilson Lumpkin and John Kennedy (appointed from Tennessee October 25 to replace William Carroll, who was ill) reported, March 23, that in January there had gathered at New Echota a company of about 600 Cherokees who wished to avail themselves of "that provision of the treaty which authorizes them to emigrate themselves and families." They had thereupon set out for Arkansas by land. Another group, of 466, composed of Major Ridge, his son John, their families and adherents, had left Ross's Landing on the Tennessee River, March 3, in

[41]

a flotilla of eleven flatboats lashed to two steamers. This party was the first to be emigrated by the United States Government under the Schermerhorn treaty; Dr. John S. Young was the conducting agent.

The Treaty Commission advocated withholding military protection from the Cherokees so they would the sooner be dispossessed in Georgia. Then, food, shelter, and clothing could be more effectively used as inducements to "voluntary" removal.

General Wool opposed the commission, in this and in its differentiating between the Cherokee people and their leaders, a policy the general considered unrealistic.

General Wool Asks to Be Relieved

Martin Van Buren, elected President in November and inaugurated the following March (1837) was the personal choice of his predecessor, so a change of policy was not be be expected, even though Van Buren, less forceful of character than Andrew Jackson, might be less resolute in carrying it out.

General Wool therefore asked to be relieved.

"The whole scene since I have been in this country," he wrote, "has been nothing but a heartrending one, and such a one as I would be glad to get rid of as soon as circumstances will permit. If I could, and I could not do them a greater kindness, I would remove every Indian tomorrow beyond the reach of white men, who, like vultures, are watching, ready to pounce upon their prey and strip them of everything they have or expect from the Government of the United States. Yes, sir, nineteen-twentieths, if not ninety-nine of every hundred, will go penniless to the West."

Colonel William Lindsay (with an order dated May 8 and signed by

Martin Van Buren who, as U.S. President from 1837 to 1841, ordered the disputed treaty of removal into execution.

Joel R. Poinsett, the new Secretary of War), arrived in the Nation to take command of troops.

General Wool did not, however, immediately leave the Nation. Personal contact with the commission was no longer required of him, but as Inspector General of the Army he remained a while on the scene. On June 3, in a letter to the Secretary of War, the general commented on the death of Benjamin F. Curry, the late Superintendent of Emigration (under the commissioners) and supervisor of appraising agents:

"Had Curry lived he would assuredly have been killed by the Indians. It is a truth that you have not a single agent, high or low, that has the slightest moral control over them. It would be wise if persons appointed to civil stations here could be taken from among those who have had nothing to do with making the late treaty."

The War Department Is Worried

Secretary of War Poinsett, disturbed by the continued refusal of Cherokees to accept the treaty as valid and binding upon them, sent new orders to Colonel Lindsay. If John Ross attempted further to incite his people against removal, he was to be "arrested" and delivered to civil authorities.

Chief Ross called for the National Council to convene July 31.

Colonel Lindsay was ordered to attend the Council and "correct any misstatements" by Ross concerning the treaty.

Secretary Poinsett, distrustful and exasperated at the latitude Army officers seemed to allow themselves in construing orders, then sent a civilian, John Mason, Jr., to observe and report. Mason, although a civilian appointee and special agent, reported, on September 25:

"The chiefs and better informed part of the Nation are convinced that they cannot retain their country. But opposition to the treaty is unanimous and irreconcilable. They say it cannot bind them because they did not make it; that it was made by a few unauthorized individuals; that the Nation was not a party to it. . . . They retain the forms of their government in their proceedings among themselves, though they have had no election since 1830, the chiefs and headmen then in power having been authorized to act until their government shall again be regularly constituted. [The State of Georgia had prevented Cherokee elections within the State's boundaries.] Under this arrangement John Ross retains the post of Principal Chief. . . . The influence of this chief is unbounded and unquestioned. The whole Nation of eighteen thousand persons is with him, the few, about three hundred, who made the treaty, having left the country. It is evident, therefore, that Ross and his party are in fact the Cherokee Nation. . . . Many who were opposed to the treaty have emigrated to secure rations, or because of fear of an outbreak. . . . The officers

[44]

say that, with all his power, Ross cannot, if he would, change the course he has heretofore pursued and to which he is held by the fixed determination of his people. He dislikes being seen in conversation with white men, and particularly with agents of the Government. Were he, as matters now stand, to advise the Indians to acknowledge the treaty, he would at once forfeit their confidence and probably his life. Yet though unwavering in his opposition to the treaty, Ross's influence has constantly been exerted to preserve the peace of the country, and Colonel Lindsay says that he (Ross) alone stands at this time between the whites and bloodshed. The opposition to the treaty on the part of the Indians is unanimous and sincere, and it is not a mere political game played by Ross for the maintenance of his ascendency in the tribe."

Border Whites Grow More Impatient

General Wool, still in the Cherokee Nation as the summer waned, again found himself in conflict with civil authorities.

The Governor and the Legislature of Alabama had, on July 3, sent the War Department a protest, charging the general with "usurping powers of the civil courts," and challenging his authority to evict white intruders from Cherokee soil.

General Wool, ordered to appear before a military court at Knoxville, Tennessee, in September, was there acquitted. He promptly reaffirmed his order to the Army that Cherokees were to be protected in their persons and property until May 23, 1838, and that all intrusions before then would be resisted.

Newspapers of north Georgia intensified their campaign of threats and exhortation. Invaders in large numbers got past the inadequate protection of too few Federal troops. Dispossessed Cherokees trudged north with their families into Tennessee. Units of Georgia militia stationed along the border insulted Federal troops, and threatened to drive them out along with the Cherokees. Militia units attempted to interfere with Army evictions of white intruders who had dispossessed Cherokees. White civilians taunted soldiers and Cherokees, stole movable property from both, destroyed Cherokee crops, and "blundered" into the way of troop movements, blocking roads and bridges, delaying ferries.

1838, the Year of Removal Begins

United States Government agents had by the first of this year dispatched westward 2,103 (mostly dispossessed) Cherokees, of whom 1,282 had moved themselves (as reported by the Secretary of War, to James K. Polk, Speaker of the House of Representatives, January 8, 1838).

William C. Dawson, a Congressman from Georgia, had, on January 2, proposed a resolution directing the Secretary of War to supply the House with certain information on the Cherokees: the numbers already moved, the disposition of the remainder, the military force entrusted with ensuring compliance to the treaty, and the Government's plans for executing it.

Horace Everett, of Vermont, a member of the Committee on Indian Affairs, moved to amend this resolution by adding: "And that the President be requested to lay before this House copies of all documents relating to the regulation of the late treaty with the Cherokee Indians, and of all communications of the Cherokee Indians relative thereto."

Henry A. Wise, of Virginia, declared that with only the documents readily available he would not fail to convince any jury, even if it included the Congressmen from Georgia, that the treaty was a fraud.

[46]

Mr. Dawson replied that ratification of the treaty had closed the issue, and that further study of it would be an "exercise in irrelevance." Mr. Everett's amendment was voted upon and defeated.

Public Opinion Is Aroused

Eastern newspapers intensified their attacks on the treaty. Papers in Tennessee and Kentucky approved its purpose while deploring it as an "improper instrument." Congressmen continued their attacks. Foreign observers commented cynically about "a government founded upon such lofty principles" having its "deviations exposed to public scrutiny."

John Ross laid before the United States Senate, February 22, a new memorial signed by 15,665 Cherokees, asking that the Schermerhorn treaty be set aside and consideration given to a redress of grievances. This memorial was rejected, March 26, by a vote of 36 to 10.

Citizens of New York State petitioned Congress to reexamine the treaty and its negotiation. The House of Representatives declined, March 28, by a vote of 102 to 75.

The Cherokees, adamantly maintaining that no treaty of removal existed, still made no preparations for moving.

Military Preparations Are Ordered

General Winfield Scott, on April 6, was placed in command of troops in the Cherokee Nation, to which were now to be added a regiment of artillery, a regiment of infantry, and six companies of dragoons.

[47]

General Winfield Scott, commander of all federal troops and state militia in the Cherokee removal, was a towering figure, six feet five inches tall. Fifty-two years old at the time, he was probably about ten years younger than he is pictured here in his uniform of the Mexican War period.

General Scott was further authorized to call upon the governors of the four states involved to provide militia and volunteers not exceeding 4,000 men.

The President Offers a Compromise

Public opinion was becoming so hostile that President Van Buren offered, subject to the approval of Congress and of the governors and legislatures of the states concerned, to allow the Cherokees two more years before being required to emigrate.

Both sides of the controversy declared that this proposal, even if approved, would solve nothing.

Governor Gilmer, of Georgia, wrote the President:

"I can give it no sanction whatever. The proposal could not be carried into effect but in violation of the rights of this State. . . . It is necessary that I should know whether the President intends that the Indians shall be maintained in their occupancy by an armed force in opposition to the rights of the owners of the soil. If such be the intention, a direct collision between the authorities of this State and the General Government must ensue. My duty will require that I shall prevent any interference whatever by the troops with the rights of the State and its citizens. I shall not fail to perform it."

The President Yields to a Governor

Secretary of War Poinsett quickly assured Governor Gilmer that the President was determined upon removal of the Cherokees at the earliest date practicable. He did not doubt that it could be accomplished in the present season.

General Scott arrived in the Cherokee Nation, setting up headquarters at New Echota. On May 10, he issued a proclamation:

"Cherokees: — The President of the United States has sent me with a powerful Army to cause you, in obedience to the treaty of 1835, to join that part of your people who are already established in prosperity on the other side of the Mississippi. Unhappily the two years allowed for that purpose you have suffered to pass away without making any preparations to follow, and now the emigration must be commenced in haste, but, I hope, without disorder. I have no power, by granting a further delay, to correct the error you have committed. The full moon of May is already on the wane, and before another shall have passed away every Cherokee, man, woman, and child, in these States, must be in motion to join their brethren in the far West. . . . My troops already occupy many positions

[49]

Ross's Landing, twenty-six years after it was used as a main staging area for the removal of the Cherokees westward. In this picture, taken in 1864, it has become the town of Chattanooga, Tennessee, and a Civil War base of supply for General Sherman's armies in his push to Atlanta.

in the country you are to abandon, and thousands and thousands are approaching from every quarter to render resistance and escape alike hopeless...."

Militia units were now arriving from Tennessee, Georgia, North Carolina, and Alabama, increasing the forces under General Scott to 9,494 men.

Stockades were being erected at strategic locations. Steamboats were being chartered. Barges were being constructed and brought to Ross's and Gunter's Landings on the Tennessee River.

Cherokees watched, and listened, stoical, incredulous, too civilized to believe that "civilized" people so very like themselves would ever do to them what seemed about to be done. In a barbarian land perhaps, but in America? Never. Thousands of white people all around them were their own relatives, by shared ancestry and by marriage.

Chief John Ross, on May 18, offered the United States Government a new proposal. He was told that the treaty of 1835 would be "construed with every liberality," that title to the western lands would be "secured by patent to the Cherokees," but no proposal for a new treaty could be entertained.

The Daily National Intelligencer, a Washington newspaper, on May 22, 1838, carried on its editorial page a long article signed "Veritas." The writer must have had access to confidential files in the War Department, for his article was composed almost entirely of excerpts quoted from official reports and letters pertaining to the treaty, many of which had not previously been published.

Opinion against the treaty, attacks upon it in and out of government, rose to a new high.

May 23, 1838—the Roundup Begins

Precisely on the day, two years after the treaty was ratified, military units deployed all over the Cherokee Nation sent out squads, armed with rifles and bayonets, and with orders to take into custody every Cherokee that could be found. Without a warning knock the doors of homes were thrust open, the residents driven out, formed into platoons with their neighbors and marched off to the stockades. Planters and tradesmen were caught at their work or going about their business in the towns, their property thereby abandoned on the spot.

Some officers of militia, themselves planters and tradesmen in private life, handed over property to relatives, or auctioned it off, and bargained for land claims, offering the evicted owner a little time in which his family could pack some things, a "favor" in exchange for a "debt" lien on the real estate being evacuated.

White civilian marauders followed close behind the military, stealing everything they could get their hands on, fighting each other over the spoils. There were fist fights, eye gougings, pistol duels, knife battles, gang brawls, in which contesting parties kicked, bit, clawed, carved, shot, and clubbed each other, often to find that someone else had meanwhile sneaked away with the loot. Wagons hired by the Army to haul clothing, bedding, and cooking utensils, from Cherokee homes to the stockades, were seized by roving bands of white men, looted on the spot, or driven off by a member of the band after the teamster had been disposed of.

On the better plantations, men with picks and shovels opened graves in family burial grounds, hoping to find silver and gold ornaments thought to have been buried with the dead.

A gang of brothers and cousins, believing all the exaggerated stories about "rich Cherokees," seized a manor house and wrecked it searching for "hidden treasure." A fire got started in the debris and the whole thing went up in flames.

Two colonels of the Georgia militia dueled with pistols from room to room of a plantation house. One was killed, his body tumbling out the dining room window into the shrubbery; the "winner" was blinded in one eye and permanently crippled.

The Cherokees, in their last acts before eviction from their old homes, were often strange as they were pathetic. One woman picked up a pan of corn and fed her chickens, then, weeping, she put on her bonnet, collected her children and led them away, never to return. Another woman, having washed and dried her dishes, insisted upon putting them carefully in her cupboard before she would leave. An ancient grandfather had his family kneel in prayer, as the soldiers, embarrassed and awkwardly respectful, stood waiting; then the old man locked all the doors, as marauders crashed in at the rear.

Mothers gave birth along the roadsides, as hundreds of Cherokees, soldiers, militiamen, white civilians clustered about, stood watching, curious, embarrassed, some trying to hide their shame with ribald humor that drew no laughs.

The great processions would move on, platoons of prisoners under heavy guard, hundreds of trudging feet raising clouds of dust, and gradually, slowly, getting smaller in the distance, they would pass from view round a bend in the road, now hidden by trees, or disappear over the top of a hill, a light reddish haze upon the crest showing that another contingent of Cherokees had seen the last of their native soil.

Birth of a Legend

Stories of the Cherokee roundup were told by the hundreds, and repeated over and over again, by the soldiers, by the militiamen, by white civilians, by news reporters, by the victims, to find their way into print and be circulated in America and abroad as parts of the larger story of the removal. Three-quarters of a century later, elderly Cherokees were passing on to their children, grandchildren, and great-grandchildren, the many-storied legend they had heard and repeated so many times they were no longer sure of just what they, as children, had personally experienced or what they had been told.

The Army acted upon the whole as could be expected of a military force subject to immediate and continuing discipline. But the militia units were no more susceptible of discipline than are temporary forces anywhere at any time.

The Reverend Evan Jones (whose reprimands by the Army for "meddling" and "agitating" in the past would not have inclined him to bias in its favor), writing from Camp Hetzel, near Cleveland, Tennessee,

June 16, to the *Baptist Missionary Magazine*, admitted: "It is only justice to say, that, at this station (and I learn that the same is true of some others) the officer in charge treats his prisoners with great respect and indulgence. But the fault lies somewhere. They are prisoners, without a crime to justify the fact."

Also, the militia units, deficient as many were in matters of discipline, did have some officers and men who performed as humanely as the task would permit.

A Georgia volunteer, who years afterward became a colonel in the Confederate Army, declared: "I fought through the War between the States, and have seen men shot to pieces by the thousands, but the Cherokee Removal was the cruelest work I ever knew."

Roundup Completed, Removal Begins

Completion of the roundup was officially announced on June 17, twenty-five days after it had begun. It was completed in Georgia by June 5, with 8,000 Cherokees in the stockades, but many had slipped across the state line into Tennessee. Some again evaded arrest by fleeing to the mountains, but except for those few (in proportion to the total captured), the entire Nation was in custody by June 15. Militia units, released as they cleared their assigned areas, were already gone by the 17th.

Removal of the Cherokees from their homeland was hardly begun when temporary suspension became almost imperative. Spring rainfall had been less than normal, then followed weeks of dry weather which, though favorable to the roundup, was less so to removal.

The first contingent of Cherokee emigrants, about 800, conducted by Lieutenant Edward Deas, had, on June 6, eleven days before the official end of the roundup, left Ross's Landing, on the Tennessee River,

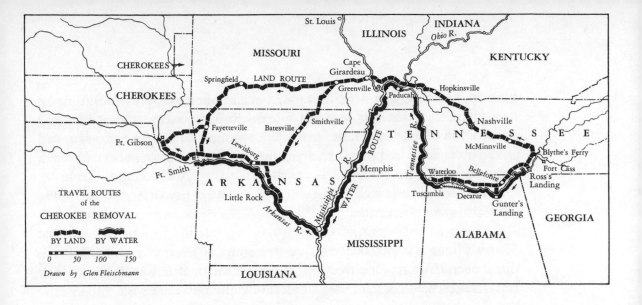

aboard a steamer and six flatboats, lashed three to a side. At Decatur, Alabama, at six in the evening of the 9th, the emigrants were disembarked to travel by rail past Muscle Shoals (not navigable in such a dry season). They camped for the night, then boarded two trains, with a total of thirty-two cars (all that could be drawn by their locomotives), but they were so crowded the lieutenant dismissed twenty-three soldiers of the guard. The first trainload, arriving as Tuscumbia in midafternoon, boarded a steamer and flatboats, and set out for Waterloo. The second trainload, on its arrival at Tuscumbia, had to pitch camp and await river transportation. Without the guard that had been dismissed, the Cherokees, who had had to be driven onto the boats at Ross's Landing, now found it easy to escape. Over a hundred fled to the woods. The remainder were carried next morning by keelboat and steamer to Waterloo, about thirty miles downriver, where the two parties, reunited, boarded the steamboat *Smelter* and two large double-decked keelboats. By the following day, when they reached Paducah, Kentucky, only 489 were left of the original 800.

The second contingent, of about 875 Cherokees, conducted by Lieutenant R. H. K. Whitely, had left Ross's Landing on June 13, also aboard

[55]

a steamer and six flatboats. It stopped at Brown's Ferry to pick up two more flatboat loads, but some prisoners escaped. Except those who had got separated from their families in the roundup and sought to be reunited with them, none had given their names, nor would they accept clothing that was purchased for them. At each stop, many escaped, and, this being the fever season, especially hard on children and the elderly, the party was further reduced by deaths.

A third contingent, of about 1,070, had left Ross's Landing on June 17, by wagon train, to board a river transport at Waterloo, but this party made even more trouble than the others. No sooner had it departed than reports were sent back, of many desertions and much sickness.

Removal Suspended

The Cherokee leaders had until now refused to cooperate, letting the United States Army prove by its use of force that the treaty was invalid. But now, to save lives, they yielded to the pressure of circumstances. Anyhow, their point was made, and the world had been so informed by the newspapers.

Cherokee leaders acting for the National Council, on June 19, two days after the third contingent had left, proposed to General Scott that emigration be suspended, on the promise that in the autumn the Indians would conduct their own removal. This proposition was condemned by officeholders, owners of steamboats and wagons, and other contractors, all of whom would profit most from a removal conducted by the Federal Government. These protests were endorsed by Andrew Jackson, who suspected "more filibustering" by John Ross, but the former President, living now in retirement at Nashville, no longed controlled the military.

General Scott, eager to detach the Army from an odious task in which no one but the victims could look good, accepted the Cherokee offer, providing they should all be on their way by September 1.

More Trouble with Emigrants en Route

The third contingent, which had left on June 17, hearing of this development, now demanded they be allowed to return. And on June 20 the Cherokee leaders, whose appeal for a stay of departure had been granted by General Scott, sent a petition to Nathan Smith, Superintendent of Emigration.

"Spare their lives," it said. "Expose them not to the killing effects of that strange climate, under the disadvantages of the present inauspicious season. . . . To this may be added the voice of our white neighbors. . . . Not longer ago than yesterday the citizens of Athens, your immediate neighbors, sent a strong and affecting petition to General Scott on our behalf signed by upwards of sixty of the principal citizens and physicians. . . . We have today heard that the citizens of Monroe and those of Blount Counties are preparing similar petitions."

This appeal Smith rejected.

The third contingent was joined by Superintendent Smith, June 25, at Bellefonte, Alabama, where he found that over a hundred had escaped. "The remainder," he wrote, "made application to me to be suffered to return to the agency and remain until fall. As they would have traveled over 120 miles, their health improving and they well provided with transportation and subsistance, I ditermined they should go on and so informed them. Shortly after which 300 of them threw their baggage out of the waggons, took it and broke for the woods and many of the balance refused to put their baggage into the waggons, or go any further and shewed much ill nature. . . . I requested the Captain of the Town Com-

[57]

pany to call out his men and aid me in starting them which he very promptly did, and we succeeded in getting off all that was left about 10 o'clock. A part of those who broke off in the morning was found and made to return. I put the party in charge of Capt. Drane of the Army and called on the citizens for 30 volunteers to accompany him to Waterloo. They turned out immediately and I had the Capt. to muster them into Sirvice for 30 days unless sooner discharged. As verry many of this party were about naked, barefoot and suffering with fatigue although they had not traveled over 9 miles pr. day, I ditermined to purchase some Clothing, Domestic for tents & shoes, &c., &c., and issue to them which was done on the 26 ult. They rested on that day in the evening of which I called as many of the aged and infirm and their Families as would go by water to Waterloo and took them to the river, put them on bord of the boat engaged in the upper contract and landed them next morning at Decatur, where I learned Lieut. Whitely's party were yet at Tuscumbia. I followed on and overtook him and party at Waterloo all dooing verry well, and getting on bored of the boats to leave which they did ot 10 o'c on 30 uto."

The foregoing account of the third contingent was written by Nathan Smith, July 3, to Lieutenant Joseph W. Harris, who was keeping a journal of the Cherokee emigration.

The second contingent, Lieutenant R. H. K. Whitely's party, which Nathan Smith was now accompanying and to which he referred as "all dooing verry well," had lost 25 Indians by desertion, one child had died and there was one birth, before it had reached Decatur. There, on June 20, one old woman died. The next morning as they were leaving aboard two trains, a man was killed by the cars when his hat blew off and he tried to catch it. At Tuscumbia, where they had to wait several days for shallow-draft boats to carry them over Colbert Shoals, two children died. While encamped opposite Waterloo to wait for the steamboat *Smelter*, three more children died, there was another birth, and 118 Indians escaped. After Smith joined the contingent another child died before they arrived at

[58]

Paducah, Kentucky. When the boats entered the Arkansas River, July 4, two more children died, and one child the next day. At Little Rock the emigrants were transferred to the *Tecumseh*, a steamboat of shallower draft, and Superintendent Smith returned on the *Smelter* to Waterloo.

Of the third contingent Smith now wrote from here, July 12, to Lieutenant Harris, that 76 more Indians had escaped before the party arrived at Waterloo, and "they continued to desert some almost every night until we put them on bord of the boats. These people will have over 300 miles to travel to reach their old homes, and many of them women and children must suffer extremely for want of something to eat &c." Also, before this party had reached Waterloo four children and one adult had died.

Nathan Smith predicted in this letter, that "of the 3,000 which I wrote you from the Agency had left in three parties, not over 2,000 will reach their new home, and all for want of a few armed men as a guard which I have politely asked the Military for but could not get them agreeably to my wish."

Some Emigrants at Last Arrive

Of all three contingents Nathan Smith wrote a final account upon his arrival in the West.

The first contingent, under Lieutenant Edward Deas, having reached Paducah with only 489 of the original 800, had no more losses, and there had not been a single death since they left Ross's Landing. Checked in at Fort Smith, Indian Territory, on June 19, they had made the journey in thirteen days.

The second contingent, under Lieutenant Whitely, reached Little Rock on July 12, transferred to the shallow-draft steamer *Tecumseh*, but thirty miles upriver it grounded on Benson's Bar, near Lewisburg. Scouting the countryside for wagons, the lieutenant's assistants found twenty-three. The party got under way again on the 20th, but left 80 sick persons, with attendants, to follow the next day, after more wagons were hired. The weather was so hot they traveled only from dawn to noon. The death rate was three, four, and five a day. In the long drought water was scarce. Food was bad. The rough, rocky roads, the dust stirred up by the horses, oxen, and wagons, added to the misery of the sick. On August 1 they pitched camp at Lee's Creek, and "did not move this day, the party needing rest and more than half sick. It was impossible to prevent their eating quantities of green peaches and corn — consequently the flux raged among them and carried off some days as high as six and seven." Four days later they entered the Cherokee Nation West and camped near the head of Lee's Creek, where the emigrants were delivered to the receiving officer, Captain Stephenson. Of the 1,000 in this party who had left the Nation East, 602 arrived, 72 had died (within three weeks), and the rest had escaped.

The third contingent, under Captain Drane and accompanied by Nathan Smith, entered the Arkansas River on July 20. The water was now so shallow the steamboat *Smelter* had to stop sixty-five miles below Little Rock, and the *Tecumseh* was brought down to take the emigrants on. From Little Rock they traveled by land, experiencing hardships much the same as did the second contingent, and arrived with 722 of the 1,070 who had left Ross's Landing.

Smith's prediction, July 12, that of the 3,000 who had started west in the three contingents not over 2,000 would reach their new home, was proved correct and with margin to spare. Only 1,813 arrived.

Degradation and Death in the Stockades

General Scott reported, June 22, to Secretary of War Joel R. Poinsett, that he had 2,500 Cherokees in stockades at Ross's Landing; 3,000 at the Cherokee Agency encampment (covering ten square miles near Calhoun, Tennessee); 1,250 in two camps between these points; 1,500 were being escorted to these camps; and 2,000 to 3,000 were at interior locations waiting to be moved into the staging area.

All these camps had been hastily thrown together, intended to be occupied just a few days until emigrants could be moved out. Only at Ross's Landing, where a few tents and sheds had been erected, was there any shelter. All sanitation facilities were primitive: slit trenches at opposite corners of stockades and hidden by tarpaulins on pole frames. Camps reeked of excrement and the sour smell of quicklime, flies passed from excrement to food being served. Water supplies during the hot dry weather were inadequate when not actually dangerous. Measles, fevers, whooping cough, chicken pox, dysentery, cholera, swept through the stockades killing Cherokees by the hundreds. Babies were born with almost no chance of survival.

Where to Place the Blame?

Congressmen blamed each other: one side was blamed for ratifying a fraudulent treaty, the other for encouraging the Cherokees to believe they would not have to move. Georgians blamed the Cherokees for not moving during the two-year period of grace. The Army blamed the politicians and the dry weather. Cherokees blamed Andrew Jackson (now living in retirement) for having started in motion a machine which no one of sufficient authority had the courage to stop.

The Senate was criticized for terminating Cherokee occupancy in the East on May 23 — for no better reason than its being exactly two years after the treaty was ratified. It was said that a more favorable date could have been chosen.

But if the treaty is accepted as valid (which ratification at least inferred), two years would seem to have been sufficient time in which the Cherokees would move at their convenience. If the ratifying Senators knew the treaty would have to be executed by force (a cynical, silent recognition that it was not a treaty), May 23 still would seem as favorable a date as any. Removal of such large numbers eight or nine hundred miles (depending on the mode of travel), and subsisting them on the journey and at their destination, would have presented problems, as all Army officers know, even if every person to be moved had been a soldier, trained, indoctrinated, and subject to military discipline. Any season would have presented its own peculiar problems. In early spring, floods or mud would have complicated any mode of travel. Winter would have exposed the emigrants to cold, rain, and snow. And since a migration of this size, over such a distance, would have extended beyond one season, it would seem that summer and early autumn (when roads and waterways usually were at their best, forage for livestock most plentiful, people could sleep on the ground with the least discomfort, and reach their destination in time to erect shelter before winter) should have been the most favorable seasons — if Nature had cooperated. That it did not, was hardly the fault of those who had set the date, whatever else they might be censured for.

Cherokees Organize Their Own Removal

The Cherokees, in accord with their proposal which induced General Scott to suspend emigration until autumn, now prepared to remove themselves.

John Ross, with the sanction of General Scott, convened the Council, at Rattlesnake Springs, two miles from Calhoun, Tennessee, and the agency. They voted to retain their present constitution and laws upon arriving in the West, passed a resolution once more denouncing the treaty and asserting that compliance under compulsion did not mean they now recognized it as valid; after which they set to work drawing up a plan of organization for the removal.

Emigrants were to be divided into fourteen parties, of about 1,000 persons each. Leaders were chosen, a police force organized, overland routes were mapped out.

The cost of removal was now estimated at about 16 cents a person and 40 cents a horse or ox, per day; 500 horses or oxen for each 1,000 persons; $65.88 a person for the whole journey. Congress had not authorized so much for this purpose, assuming that about half the emigrants would walk. But disabilities from sickness and disease had increased the needs for transportation. Unable to get it any other way, the Cherokee leaders finally offered to let the additional expense be deducted from the purchase price of their homeland.

"As their own funds pay it," said the Commissioner of Indian Affairs, "and it was insisted on by their own confidential agents, it was thought it could not be rejected."

General Scott approved, July 25, the plans drawn by the Cherokee leaders, exodus to begin by September 1, the last contingent to leave by October 20. The Army was ordered to assemble 645 wagons, 5,000 horses and oxen, and water transport for the most seriously ill. Winter clothing was purchased for those who had lost theirs in the roundup. The Cherokees asked for soap, which the Army had not included in supplies for the journey, so this cost also was deducted from their funds, and soap was purchased in amounts of two pounds per emigrant.

On August 30, two caravans with a total of 2,500 persons started out from the agency, but stopped, at Blythe's Ferry (on the Tennessee River, near the mouth of the Hiwassee), after going about twenty miles. Drought still prevailing, advance agents reported back that in mountain streams the flow of water was insufficient for livestock in large numbers and for operating gristmills (whole grain did not become wormy, so flour and meal were ground as needed). Forage also was scant.

Removal was again postponed, until end of drought.

Removal at Last Gets Under Way

October 1, after two good rains, the caravans began to move, with John Ross now instead of Nathan Smith supervising and scheduling departures.

United States Treaty Commissioners, Wilson Lumpkin (of Georgia), and John Kennedy (of Tennessee), were responsible for settling all claims for damages or loss of Cherokee property caused by the removal, as well as claims against Indians for debts owed to whites, but a great many emigrants left without having these matters settled. Councils were held in camps along the way, and messages were sent back to John Ross, expressing fear that compensation for losses would not be paid and that whites would present fraudulent claims which individual Cherokees would have no chance to refute.

Those who had gone earlier and not under compulsion (the Ridge party and others who had abandoned hope of remaining in their homeland) had obtained adjustments promptly. But of those who left in the mass exodus, many had still declined to give their names, fearing that it would be construed as acceptance of the treaty.

During October nine caravans left. Remaining were enough to make up four. And one party, those in poorest health, would go by water, personally supervised by John Ross.

November 4 the last caravan moved out. The Ross boat then left Ross's Landing.

Complacency in High Offices

President Martin Van Buren, December 4, 1838, in his Message to both Houses of Congress (four months before the last contingent would arrive in the West), announced:

"It affords me sincere pleasure to be able to apprise you of the entire removal of the Cherokee Nation of Indians to their new homes west of the Mississippi. The measures authorized by Congress with a view to the long-standing controversy with them have had the happiest effects, and they have emigrated without any apparent reluctance. . . ."

The Secretary of War, Joel R. Poinsett, in his report (dated November 28 but which accompanied the President's Message to Congress), wrote:

"The generous and enlightened policy evinced in the measures adopted by Congress towards that people, was ably and judiciously carried into effect, . . . in every instance with promptness and praiseworthy humanity. . . . They [Cherokees] departed with alacrity under the guidance of their own chiefs. The arrangements for this, . . although somewhat costly to the Indians themselves, met the entire approbation of the Department, as it was deemed of the last importance that the Cherokees

[65]

should remove to the West voluntarily, and that, on their arrival, . . they should recur to the manner in which they had been treated with kind and grateful feelings. Humanity, no less than sound policy dictated this course. . . . It will always be gratifying to reflect that this has been effected, not only without violence, but with every proper regard for the feelings and interests of that people."

Dissent and Refutation

President Van Buren and Secretary Poinsett were deluged with verbal brickbats, in Congress and in the press. A long editorial, for example, in the *Daily National Intelligencer*, December 8, answered point by point the President's Message, the bulk of which had consisted of a long defense and justification of the Government Indian Policy generally. The President had asserted that government dealings with the Indian tribes had been "just and friendly throughout," and that the United States had "fulfilled in good faith all their treaty obligations with the Indian tribes."

"Before we can claim for our Government," the editorialist wrote, "the credit of having dealt 'justly' with the Indians throughout, we must sponge from the tablet of memory the enforcement of a treaty with the Seminoles which the Seminoles never made; the removal of the Creeks from their lands in the face of a solemn covenant; the refusal to fulfill our treaty stipulations with the Cherokees for ten years, and the final enforcement of a treaty to which they never assented, and which never could have been carried into execution but by an armed force which it was in vain for them to contend against."

The editorial erred on the side of leniency. *Every* treaty between the United States and the Indians was dishonored by the stronger signatory, after it obtained what it wanted and had nothing more to gain by fulfill-

[66]

ing its obligation, or when it hoped to secure a new treaty on the pretext that standing commitments could not be fulfilled.

Bleak Reality with the Caravans

The route of this emigration, whether starting from Calhoun or Ross's Landing in Tennessee, or Gunter's Landing in Alabama, passed through Nashville, continued northwest through Hopkinsville, Kentucky, crossed the Mississippi River at Cape Girardeau, Missouri, or Green's Ferry, then proceeded southwest to Fort Smith and Fort Gibson, Indian Territory.

After the drought had broken there was plenty of rain.

The *Nashville Banner* reported that roads traveled by the emigrants were in wretched condition, many places axle deep in mud. The last con-

Fort Gibson was the western terminal point for emigrants in the Cherokee removal. This replica, now open to tourists, stands on the site of the original, at Fort Gibson, Oklahoma. (Photo by author)

The Reverend Jesse Bushyhead, Cherokee minister. Just after he and his wife crossed the Mississippi River in January, 1839, a daughter was born to them. (From a portrait by C. B. King, courtesy of his granddaughter, Mrs. J. W. McSpadden)

tingent, numbering about 1,800, passed through Nashville on December 2, nearly a month after it had started from Calhoun. Emigrants were suffering much from cold.

The *Arkansas Gazette*, December 20, reported of one contingent that "owing to their exposure to the inclemency of the weather, and many of them being destitute of shoes and other necessary articles of clothing, about 50 of them have died." On January 2 the same newspaper reported on a caravan of 1,200 that passed through Smithville, on December 12: "They have the measles and whooping cough among them and there is an average of four deaths per day."

The *New York Observer*, January 26, 1839, carried an article signed by "A Native of Maine, traveling in the Western Country," which gave this account:

"... On Tuesday evening we fell in with a detachment of the poor Cherokee,.. about eleven hundred Indians — sixty waggons — six hundred

[68]

horses, and perhaps forty pairs of oxen. We found them in the forest camped for the night by the roadside, . . under a severe fall of rain accompanied by heavy wind. With their canvas for a shield from the inclemency of the weather, and the cold wet ground for a resting place, after the fatigue of the day, they spent the night. Many of the aged Indians were suffering extremely from the fatigue of the journey and the ill health consequent upon it, . . several were then quite ill, and one aged man we were informed was then in the last struggles of death. . . .

"We met several detachments in the southern part of Kentucky on the 4th, 5th, and 6th of December. . . . The last detachment we passed on the 7th embraced rising two thousand Indians with horses and mules in proportion. The forward part of the train we found just pitching their tents for the night, and notwithstanding some thirty or forty waggons were already stationed, the road was literally filled with the procession for about three miles. . . . We learned from the inhabitants on the road where the Indians passed, that they buried fourteen and fifteen at every stopping place. . . .

"The Indians as a whole carry in their countenances everything but the appearance of happiness. . . . Most of them seemed intelligent and refined. . . . Some Cherokees are wealthy and travel in style.

"One lady passed on in her hack in company with her husband, apparently with as much refinement and equipage as any mother of New England; and she was a mother too and her youngest child about three years old was sick in her arms, and all she could do was make it comfortable as circumstances would permit. She could only carry her dying child in her arms a few miles farther, and then she must stop in a stranger-land and consign her much loved babe to the cold ground, and that too without ceremony, and pass on with the multitude. . . .

"When I passed the last detachment of those suffering exiles and thought that my countrymen had thus expelled them from their native soil and their much loved homes, . . I turned from the sight with feelings which language cannot express and 'wept like childhood' then. . . .

"When I read in the President's Message that he was happy to inform the Congress that the Cherokees were peaceably and without reluctance removed — and remember that it was on the 4th day of December, when not one of the detachments had reached their destination; and that a large majority had not made even half their journey, I wished the President could have been there that day in Kentucky with myself, and have seen the comfort and the willingness with which the Cherokees were making their journey. But I forbear, full well I know that many prayers have gone up to the King of Heaven from Maine in behalf of the poor Cherokees."

The caravans arrived at Fort Smith, Indian Territory, January 4, 7, 10, February 2, 23, 27, March 1, 2, 5, 14, 18, 24, 25, 1839.

Chief John Ross and his family, with the last party of Cherokees to leave their homeland, arrived at Little Rock, February 1, aboard the steamboat *Victoria*. The party numbered 228, many of whom sickness had prevented from starting on the journey by land. The Ross family were mourning the death of their wife and mother, Elizabeth Brown Henley Ross, known to her friends as "Quatie." She had died as the boat approached Little Rock, and was buried there, in the cemetery lot of a family friend, General Albert Pike.

The Summing Up

Total figures on the Cherokee Removal had to be approximate, so many refused to give their names and had to be counted. No doubt some were missed in the various countings and some were counted more than once.

Nathan Smith, United States Superintendent of Emigration, had, before the treaty time limit expired, removed 821 dispossessed who were

A group of Eastern Cherokee councilmen, descendants of those who escaped the removal. (Charles Phelps Cushing)

willing to accept compensation for losses and be moved by the Government. And 1,282 dispossessed had accepted compensation and removed themselves. After the roundup Nathan Smith removed about 3,000; but, while those who died on the way and those who arrived were accounted for, of those who escaped some were recaptured and included in later figures. In October, Nathan Smith sent west, conducted by Lieutenant Edward Deas, about 700 who refused to move under the direction of John Ross.

Those who had evaded capture and escapees who evaded recapture were said to number 1,046, but such a seemingly precise figure for

Councilmen of the Western Cherokees, descendants of those who made the journey west. (Charles Phelps Cushing)

those least amenable to accurate counting would seem to be of dubious credibility.

John Ross recorded that 13,149 emigrated under his direction. Of these, 11,504 were received by Captain Stephenson at Fort Smith. But Disbursing Officer Captain Page counted 11,721.

Cherokees in the Nation East before the removal numbered about 19,000 (the total number 18,952 included some figures that were only estimates). About 2,500 died in the roundup and in the stockades. About 16,500 left the old Nation (many of whom escaped and hid in the mountains), and about 1,500 were buried on the journey. So, in the ten months between roundup in the East and last arrivals in the West about 4,000 died. There were about 475 births, but many of the newborn died.

The Commissioner of Indian Affairs wrote in his report:

"The case of the Cherokees is a striking example of the liberality of the Government in all its branches. . . . A retrospect of the last eight months in reference to this numerous and more than ordinarily enlightened tribe cannot fail to be refreshing to well constituted minds. . . . If our acts have been generous, they have not been less wise and politic. . . . Good feeling has been preserved, and we have quietly and gently transported 18,000 friends to the west bank of the Mississippi."

Considerably more than "18,000" had lived in the old Nation, but a great many less arrived at Fort Smith.

However, President Van Buren had assured the Cherokees that security in their new lands was "guaranteed" to them by the United States, and that they would have "exclusive possession of that country *forever*, exempt from all intrusions by white men, with ample provisions for their security against external violence and internal dissension" — an assurance which at least had the ring of familiarity and was sanctioned by precedent and usage.

All previous treaties had contained the same assurance.

Afterword

Martin Van Buren was not elected to a second term as President of the United States. But the Whigs, who had so criticized government policy toward the Indians, did not upon accession to power themselves make any notable changes in it.

The Cherokees now assembled in the West, still not united, were of three parties: the Old Settlers (who had emigrated in previous years), the

A painting depicting the famous council meeting called by John Ross in 1843. (The Smithsonian from Cushing)

Treaty Party, and the Ross Party. Of the treaty signers, three were "executed" by persons unknown. Early in the morning of June 22, 1839, John Ridge, dragged from his bed before his household had risen, was left dead upon the ground outside his door, twenty knife wounds in his body. Elias Boudinot, in the tall, dewy prairie grass three hundred yards from his new house under construction was found dying, stabbed repeatedly and hacked about the head with a hatchet. Killed about ten o'clock was John's father and Boudinot's uncle, Major Ridge, who, over thirty years before, had been the one most responsible for enactment of the tribal law decreeing death to anyone signing away Cherokee land without authority from his people. He was also one of the "executioners" of Chief Doublehead, for that reason.

The Council, July 7, voted amnesty to the surviving treaty signers. On July 10, amnesty was granted also to the unknown "executioners."

John Ross, elected Principal Chief of the not exactly united Cherokee Nation, and continuing in office, died August 1, 1866, in Washington, where he was discussing with United States officials yet another treaty

Elias Cornelius Boudinot, son of Elias and Harriet Gold Boudinot, was born in 1835 and died in 1890. About two and a half years old when his family moved west, just before the mass removal of the Cherokee Nation, he was editor of the Cherokee Advocate, 1880–81. (New York Public Library)

Will Rogers in 1908, one year after the Cherokee Nation was dissolved in the new state of Oklahoma, and exactly 100 years after his great-great-grandfather John Rogers participated in the execution of Chief Doublehead for his having signed away Cherokee lands without authority from his people.

William W. Keeler, modern-day Principal Chief of the Cherokees, chairman of the board of Phillips Petroleum Company, and chairman of the board of the National Association of Manufacturers.

being thrust upon the Cherokees. He had served his people for over fifty years, thirty-eight as Principal Chief.

The Cherokees, with the passing years, were "persuaded," as they so often had been persuaded in the East, to sign away tract after tract of their western lands until, in 1898, under pressure by the United States, they agreed to divide their remaining lands among individual Cherokees.

In 1907, dissolved in the new State of Oklahoma, the Cherokee Nation ceased to exist as a political entity.

A Selected Bibliography

Congressional Record (bound volumes). 1831, 1832, 1833, 1834, 1835, 1836, 1837, 1838, 1839.

Dale, Edward Everett, and Litton, Gaston, eds. *Cherokee Cavaliers*. Norman: University of Oklahoma Press, 1940.

Dunbar, Seymour. *A History of Travel in America*. 4 vols. 1915.

Eaton, Rachel Caroline. *John Ross and the Cherokee Indians*. 1914.

Foreman, Grant. *Indian Removal*. 1932.

Gabriel, Ralph H. *Elias Boudinot, Cherokee, and His America*. 1941.

Gilmer, George R. *Sketches of Some of the First Settlers of Upper Georgia* (of the Cherokees and the author). Records and correspondence. 1855.

Jackson, Helen Hunt. *A Century of Dishonor*. 1885.

Lumpkin, Wilson. *The Removal of the Cherokee Indians from Georgia*. 1907.

Meserve, John Bartlett. "Chief John Ross." *Chronicles of Oklahoma*, December, 1935.

Mitchell, S. Augustus. *Traveler's Guide through the United States*. 1835.

Parker, Thomas Valentine. *The Cherokee Indians*. 1907.

Peters, Richard. "Cherokee Nation vs. State of Georgia." *United States Supreme Court Reports*, Vol. I.

———. "Worcester vs. State of Georgia." *United States Supreme Court Reports*, Vol. VI, p. 515.

Phillips, U. B. *Georgia and State Rights*.

Ross, Mrs. William P. *The Life and Times of the Hon. William P. Ross, of the Cherokee Nation*.

Royce, Charles C. *The Cherokee Nation of Indians* (Fifth Annual Report of the Bureau of Ethnology to the Secretary of the Smithsonian Institution, 1883-1884, by J. W. Powell, Director). Washington: Government Printing Office, 1887.

Smith, Calvin. *Emigrants Guide and Directory*. 1835.

Smith, James F. *The Cherokee Land Lottery*. New York: 1838.

Starkey, Marion L. *The Cherokee Nation*. 1946.

Starr, Emmet. *History of the Cherokee Indians*. 1921.

Strong, William E. *The Story of the American Board*. 1910.

Walker, Robert Sparks. *Torchlights to the Cherokees*. 1932.

Wardell, Morris J. *A Political History of the Cherokee Nation*, 1838-1907. 1938.

Index

Adair, James, 7
Adams, John Quincey, 3
Agriculture, 7, 11
Alabama:
    allegations against General Wool, 45
    Cherokee land in, 6, 9, 18
    militia, 50
    removal of Cherokees from, 3
Alphabet, Cherokee, 14-16
Arkansas Gazette, 68
Arms, surrender of, by Cherokees, 39

Baptist Missionary Magazine, 54
Bell, S. W., 33
Blackburn, Gideon, 26
Boudinot, Elias, 31-33, 34, 75
Brainerd Mission, 14
Briggs, George N., 22
Brown, James, 27

Cannon, Newton, 4
Carolinas, the, 6. *See also* North Carolina; South Carolina
Carroll, William, 24, 38, 41
Cass, Lewis, 24, 35, 40
Catawba Indians, 6

Census of 1835, of Cherokees, 12
Cherokee Indians:
    character of, 6, 50-51
        peacefulness, 38, 39, 45
    denial of rights in Georgia, 20, 22, 44
    economy of, 3, 11
    farming, 7, 11
    neighbors of, 6
    number of:
        in 1755 (estimated), 7
        1835 census, 12
        in 1838, before removal, 3, 72
        losses in removal, 3, 72-73
    society of:
        adaptation to settled life, 3-4, 9-11
        in 1830's, 12-14
        matriarchalism, 7
        at time of colonization, 6-7
    surrender of arms by, 39
    "voluntary" migration to west, 12, 19, 20
    under the Treaty, 41-42, 44, 46, 64, 70-71
Cherokee Nation:
    capital of, 17
    census of 1835, 12

[81]

[82]

Dawson, William C., 46, 47
Deas, Lieutenant Edward, 54, 59, 71
Death penalty, for unauthorized signing-away of Cherokee land, 30-31, 75
Deaths, during removal, 56, 58-59, 60, 61, 68, 69
   statistics, 3, 72-73
"Dependent nation:"
   clause in Cherokee treaty, 21
   Supreme Court interpretation of, 22
Disarmament of Cherokees, 39
Discovery, Principle of, 21
Disease, during removal, 3, 56, 60, 61, 68
Doublehead, Chief, 31, 75
Drane, Captain, 58, 60
Dunlap, General R. G., 39

Education, Cherokee, 14-17
Elections, Cherokee Nation, 17, 44
English literacy, among Cherokees, 17
Escapes, during removal, 54, 55, 56, 57, 58, 59, 60, 71
Everett, Edward, 28
Everett, Horace, 28, 46, 47
Exclusive right of purchase, 19, 21

Farming, 7, 11
Federal Government, Indian policy of:
   duplicity and ambiguity, 18-20, 29, 66-67, 73

Jacksonian policy toward Cherokees, 20, 21, 22, 23, 34
Jeffersonian policy toward Cherokees, 18-19
Report to Congress on, 65-66
treaties with Cherokees, 7, 18, 21, 22, 39, 66
treaty of removal sought, 19, 20, 23, 24-25, 35
Van Buren policy, 42, 48-51, 65-66
Whig policy, 73
Federal troops, in Cherokee Nation, 47, 49-50
   misuse of, 23, 39
   in partial Cherokee removal, 54-56, 57-60, 71
   for protection of Cherokees, 39, 45-46
   in roundup, 3, 51-52, 53-54
Florida, 6
France, 19
Frelinghuysen, Theodore, 30

Georgia:
   Cherokee land in, 6, 9, 18
   claim to western lands "relinquished" by, 18-19
   demands for federal protection, 38-39
   denial of Cherokees' rights by, 20, 22, 44
   1830 population figures, 12
   harassment of Cherokees in, 20, 22, 39, 41, 45-46

[83]

[86]

[87]

[88]